Happy
Either Way

Happy and Worried

I'm just so happy, I can't wait,

For me and Mama's special date:

We're heading to the zoo today,

To see the animals and play.

ZOO

3

As we walk into the zoo,

I share my favorite thing to do:

I blurt out, "the big giraffe!"

While Mama laughs her funny laugh.

The slide's so big, I love it so,

But there are times I just don't know:

Am I brave enough to slide?

Is it okay to run and hide?

Walking by a pane of glass,

I see a tiger roaming past,

Then it stops, right next to me,

A gorgeous animal to see.

"Mama, look way over there—

Is that a special kind of bear?"

Mama knows, 'cause she's so wise:

"It's called a sloth bear," she replies.

We keep on walking, and then soon,

We come across a big baboon!

I'm feeling just a little shy,

But Mama says, "it's saying hi!"

I take the backpack off my back,

And down we settle for a snack,

While we're munching, I confide:

"I'm scared of going down the slide."

Mama smiles and hugs me tight,

"I know you are, and that's all right,

How about you get in line?

Whatever you decide is fine."

I see a bunch of kids ahead,

and keep in mind what Mama said,

I climb the ladder to a deck,

And wait to slide straight down
the neck.

I watch the kid in front of me,

Go sailing down while shouting

"whee!"

I'm nervous and my eyes are wide,

I just don't know if I can slide.

Does she go down the slide?

No

turn to the next page

Yes

jump ahead to page 32

I take a breath, and let it out,

And think of what we talked about,

I change my mind, and turn around,

And climb the ladder toward the ground.

Mama smiles and holds me tight,

"You know what? Everything's all right,

It's hard and brave to change your mind,

Why don't we try another time?"

I sit and watch the kids awhile,

Their shouts and hollers make me smile,

We ride the carousel instead,

While dizzy feelings fill my head.

We cross a bridge that leads outside,

My heart is full, my smile is wide,

I worried, but I made it through:

A perfect Sunday at the zoo.

I take a breath, and let it out,

And think of what we talked about,

I feel excitement all around,

And down I fly right to the ground.

I see my Mama clap and cheer:

"Hooray! You overcame your fear,

You look so proud," my Mama coos,

"It's hard to know which path to
 choose."

We cross a bridge that leads outside,

My heart is full, my smile is wide,

I worried, but I made it through:

A perfect Sunday at the zoo.

Can you find a page where the little girl felt happy?

Can you make a happy face?

When have you felt happy?